W9-AUM-480

MAY 1 5 2013

OUTLAWS AND LAWMEN
· OF THE WILD WEST ·

WYATT EARP

REVISED EDITION

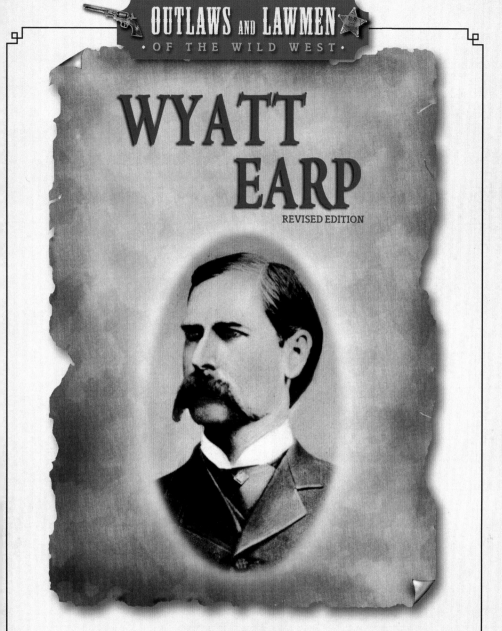

By Carl R. Green and William R. Sanford

F Enslow Publishers, Inc.
40 Industrial Road
Box 398
Berkeley Heights, NJ 07922

Cromaine District Library
3688 N. Hartland Road
PO Box 308
Hartland, MI 48353-0308
www.cromaine.org

Copyright © 2009 by Carl R. Green and William R. Sanford.

All rights reserved.

No part of this book may be reproduced by any means without the written permission of the publisher.

Original edition published in 1992.

Library of Congress Cataloging-in-Publication Data
Green, Carl R.
  Wyatt Earp / Carl R. Green and William R. Sanford. — Rev. ed.
    p. cm. — (Outlaws and lawmen of the wild West)
  Summary: "Readers will find out about the extraordinary life of Wyatt Earp, a well-known lawman of the Wild West. Includes further reading suggestions and internet addresses"—Provided by publisher.
  Includes bibliographical references and index.
  ISBN 978-0-7660-3174-6
  1. Earp, Wyatt, 1848–1929—Juvenile literature. 2. Peace officers—Southwest, New—Biography—Juvenile literature. 3. United States marshals—Southwest, New—Biography—Juvenile literature. 4. Southwest, New—Biography—Juvenile literature. 5. Tombstone (Ariz.)—History—19th century—Juvenile literature. I. Sanford, William R. (William Reynolds), 1927– II. Title.
  F786.E18G743 2009
  978'.02092—dc22
  [B]   2008010010

ISBN-10: 0-7660-3174-8

Printed in the United States of America

032013 The HF Group, North Manchester, IN

10 9 8 7 6 5 4 3 2

To Our Readers:
We have done our best to make sure all Internet Addresses in this book were active and appropriate when we went to press. However, the authors and the publisher have no control over and assume no liability for the material available on those Internet sites or on other Web sites they may link to. Any comments or suggestions can be sent by e-mail to comments@enslow.com or to the address on the back cover.

♻ Enslow Publishers, Inc., is committed to printing our books on recycled paper. The paper in every book contains 10% to 30% post-consumer waste (PCW). The cover board on the outside of each book contains 100% PCW. Our goal is to do our part to help young people and the environment too!

Interior photos: Alamy/Paris Pierce, p. 25; Alamy/Photos 12, p. 43; The Bridgeman Art Library/Private Collection, Peter Newark Western Americana, p. 11; The Bridgeman Art Library/Private Collection, Peter Newark American Pictures, p. 26; Corbis/Bettman, p. 5; CORBIS SYGMA/John Van Hasselt, pp. 18, 39, 41; Courtesy of the collections of John Rose, p. 9; The Granger Collection, New York, pp. 1, 16, 29, 30, 32; iStockphoto/spxChrome, (marshal badge), odd pages; iStockphoto/Alex Bramwell (revolver), even pages; iStockphoto/billnoll (frame), pp. 4, 14, 34; Legends of America, pp. 12, 14, 21, 23, 34, 37; Picture History, p. 7; Shutterstock/Dhoxax (background), pp. 3, 5, 8–9, 15, 21, 28–29, 35, 42–43.

Cover photo: The Granger Collection, New York (*Wyatt Earp was a tough and fearless lawman. Along with his brothers Morgan and Virgil, he cleaned up some of the toughest cowtowns in the Wild West.*)

TABLE OF CONTENTS

... **AUTHORS' NOTE** ...

This book tells the true story of a western lawman named Wyatt Earp. Wyatt was as well known a hundred years ago as film stars are now. In those days, his exploits were described in newspapers, magazines, and dime novels. More recently, Wyatt has been featured in movies and a television series. Some of the stories told about the famous lawman are fictional, but many are true. All of the events described in this book are drawn from firsthand reports.

CHAPTER ONE

THE BUNTLINE SPECIAL

In 1876, Dodge City, Kansas, was known as the toughest town on the prairies. Cowboys who herded their cattle there from Texas stayed to drink, play cards, and pick fights. The trouble grew worse after roughnecks drove the deputy marshal out of town. Marshal Deger, a slow-moving 300-pounder, could not keep the peace. To restore order, the town council sent for Wyatt Earp.

This photo of Wyatt Earp was taken in Dodge City. Dodge was just one of the tough towns Wyatt tamed.

Wyatt was a good choice. He moved in and quickly tamed Dodge's wild nightlife. Cowboys out on a wild spree backed down under Wyatt's icy stare. The young deputy marshal's success in Dodge added to his growing fame.

A few weeks later, legend tells us, Ned Buntline came to town. Buntline wrote for the popular magazines known as dime novels. He said he had come west to honor the lawmen who starred in his tales. When he met Wyatt, he gave him a special Colt six-gun. These Buntline Specials had twelve-inch barrels, four inches longer than most Colts. The guns also had carved wooden handles and fine leather holsters.

Wyatt carried the long-barreled pistol on his right hip. The gun's extra length did not slow down his fast draw. Despite his skill with a gun, Wyatt was not trigger-happy. Even when he had a pistol in his hand, he seldom shot anyone. One night, he ran into two cowboys behind a dance hall. One of them drew and fired at him, but missed. Instead of shooting back, Wyatt slammed his heavy gun against the cowboy's head. The man crumpled and fell, knocked out cold.

Cool action was Wyatt's style. He said that hitting a man on the head was better than shooting him. If asked, the cowboy would surely have agreed. After all, waking up with a headache was better than not waking up at all!

Ned Buntline was an adventurer and famous writer in the late 1800s. He gave Wyatt a special six-gun called a Buntline Special.

CHAPTER TWO

GROWING UP TO BE A LAWMAN

Wyatt Berry Stapp Earp was born in Monmouth, Illinois, on March 19, 1848. He was the fifth of eight children. His parents, Nicholas and Virginia Earp, were from Kentucky. Nicholas was trained as a lawyer, but farming was his first love. He also had a keen sense of duty. After moving to Monmouth, Nicholas served as an unpaid lawman. Then, with the outbreak of the Mexican War in 1846, he joined the U.S. Army as a captain. Wyatt was named for the officer who led his father's unit during the war.

When Wyatt was two years old, the family moved to Pella, Iowa. In those days, this was frontier country. At times, the only law was that of the six-gun. Nicholas believed it was the duty of good men to stand up for what was right. He drummed that message into the heads of his children. Nicholas also valued learning. When they outgrew the village schools, the Earp children studied at home. They also learned to stick together in good times and bad.

Nicholas was hoping to move from Iowa to California. The death in 1858 of Martha, Wyatt's older sister, delayed the move. Then, in 1861, the Civil War broke out. Nicholas, along with his three older sons—Newton, James, and Virgil—joined the Union Army. Young Wyatt had to stay home. With the help of his brothers

Wyatt's large family was close-knit, with seven brothers and sisters. He is pictured here with his mother, Virginia, when he was still a young boy.

Morgan and Warren, he planted eighty acres of corn. Army life sounded more exciting, however, and Wyatt ran off to enlist. To his surprise the first soldier he met was his father! Nicholas sent his young son back to the cornfields.

In 1864, Nicholas left the army. He loaded his family into two covered wagons and set out for the West Coast. Other families from Pella and Monmouth joined the wagon train. Wyatt, strong for his age, drove one of the wagons. It was a man's job, but he did it well. Hunting was the teenager's second duty. Thanks to his marksmanship, the party often dined on fresh game.

The long, hard trip took seven months. After crossing the Mojave Desert, the Earps settled in San Bernardino, California. Nicholas bought a ranch and later served as a county judge. He wanted Wyatt to study law, but the boy had other plans.

Young Wyatt left home and found work as a stagecoach driver. One of his stage runs was from San Bernardino to Los Angeles. Another took him across the desert to Prescott, Arizona. In 1868, he went to Wyoming to help build the Union Pacific Railroad. Wyatt soon proved he could handle the mule teams used to grade the roadbed. He also displayed a sharp head for business. After saving some money, he bought his own mule teams and hired men to drive them. When the job was done, his books showed a $2,500 profit.

In 1870, Wyatt returned to Illinois. While he was there, he wed Urilla Sutherland. Sadly, Urilla died of typhus that same year. After he buried his bride, Wyatt joined a party that was mapping the Indian Territory in

When Wyatt left home as a young man, he hired on as a stagecoach driver. This driver is traveling a route in California similar to the routes that Wyatt drove.

what is now Oklahoma. Hired as a buffalo hunter, he carried two pistols, a rifle, and a shotgun.

After the job was finished, Wyatt spent the summer of 1871 in Kansas City. He was young, footloose, and had cash in his pocket. The money paid

Cowboys drove large herds of cattle from Texas to Kansas to be shipped east by rail. While they were in town, the cowpokes hit the saloons and card tables, looking for a wild good time.

for days filled with whiskey, cards, and dance hall girls. Some reports claim that while in Indian Territory, Wyatt stole a few horses. Arrested and then set free on bond, he fled before his case came to trial.

Kansas was wide open in the years after the Civil War. Cowboys drove cattle north from Texas to meet the newly built railroads. Then, with money in their jeans, they went looking for a good time. They drank, gambled, and settled quarrels with fists and six-guns.

Lawmen tried, often in vain, to keep the peace. Arresting armed, drunken cowboys tested a man's courage. As it turned out, Wyatt Earp had that kind of nerve.

Wyatt now stood 6 feet, 2 inches tall and weighed 185 pounds. Women admired his blue eyes, straight nose, and drooping mustache. When he was angry, those blue eyes turned to ice. Like most men, he was neither all good nor all bad. Even his critics agreed that he was brave and loyal. He did not look for fights, but neither did he back down in the face of danger.

In 1873, Wyatt drifted into Ellsworth, Kansas. Cattle grazed the lush grass outside of town. At night, bands of cowboys thronged the saloons. Like most cowtowns, Ellsworth was a violent place.

One day Wyatt saw a gambler named Bill Thompson shoot the town's sheriff. As Bill fled, his brother Ben covered his escape with a shotgun. A crowd of Texans stood by, ready to back him up. The town's police officers looked at the well-armed cowboys and backed away. When Mayor Miller heard the news, he fired his gun-shy lawmen. Then he gave Wyatt a badge. "I order you to arrest Ben Thompson," the mayor said.

Wyatt knew what his father would have done. He buckled on a pair of six-guns and walked out on the dusty street. Ben watched him, shotgun in hand.

When Wyatt stood up to the well-known gunslinger Ben Thompson (above) in Ellsworth, Kansas, he earned his reputation as a tough lawman who would not back down to anyone.

As Wyatt came closer, he kept his eyes on Ben's hands. If those hands moved he was ready to draw and fire. When Wyatt reached a point fifteen yards away, Ben asked him what he wanted. Wyatt said he was there to arrest Ben or to kill him. Ben must have sensed that Wyatt meant what he said. He threw down his shotgun and raised his hands.

Wyatt's first day as a lawman in Ellsworth was also his last. A judge fined Ben Thompson just $25 and told Wyatt to give him back his guns. The judge's handling of the case told Wyatt that the town would not stand behind him. He turned in his badge and left.

Ben Thompson was well known as a gambler and a gunslinger. Word that a young lawman had faced him down spread quickly. Wyatt now had a reputation. Any town that needed a tough, fearless marshal would surely want to hire him.

CHAPTER THREE

CLEANING UP THE COWTOWNS

In 1874, cowboys were running wild in Wichita, Kansas. When Wyatt came to town, the mayor tried to hire him as deputy marshal. Wyatt did not need the job, but it was clear the town needed him. After the mayor promised to back him, Wyatt pinned on the badge. The city gave him two Colt forty-fives and $125 a month. The generous pay pleased Wyatt. Most lawmen were paid far less.

Wyatt did not waste any time. He started by hiding shotguns in a number of stores and saloons. The weapons would come in handy if a gunslinger challenged him. Wyatt knew that many Texas cowboys hated him for what he had done to Ben Thompson.

Abel "Shanghai" Pierce, a rich Texas cattle king, was staying in town. Like the cowboys who worked for him, Shanghai liked his liquor. One day, Wyatt found him weaving along the main street, yelling

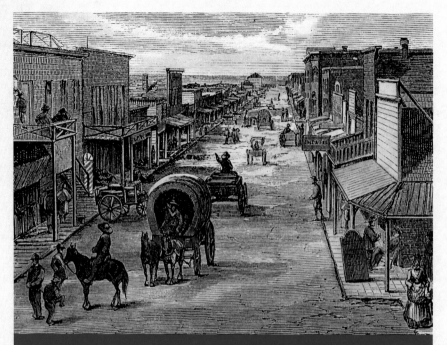

Wichita, Kansas, was the first of the wild cowtowns that Wyatt cleaned up. He arrived there in 1874, the same year an artist drew this Wichita street scene.

drunken oaths. He took Shanghai's gun away and told him to lay off the whiskey.

Before long, a crowd of angry Texans gathered on the street. They fired their guns in the air and swore they would avenge their boss. The shooting alarmed the townsfolk, who loaded their own guns. Bloodshed was in the air.

Wyatt had to act fast. He grabbed a shotgun, ran down an alley, and stepped into the street behind the mob. The quick move took the Texans by surprise.

Pointing the shotgun at their leader, Wyatt told him to put up his hands. The cowboy took one look at the shotgun—and dropped his pistol. Jolted out of his drunken fog, Shanghai ordered the others to do the same. Wyatt then marched the Texans to the courthouse. As a judge found each man guilty, Shanghai paid the $100 fines.

The cowboys were boiling mad. After vowing to get even, they picked Mannen Clements to lead them. Clements was known to be a killer. For his part, Wyatt rounded up a posse to defend the town. When a scout told him the Texans were coming, he lined his men up on the main street. Before long he saw forty cowboys crossing the bridge into town. Wyatt stepped forward to meet them.

Clements, who was holding a gun in each hand, studied the marshal. Wyatt's hands were swinging free, close to his twin six-guns. He ordered Clements to head back to his camp. Seconds ticked past as the two men stared at each other. The standoff ended when Clements slowly put his guns away. As Wyatt watched, still on guard, the cowboys walked back across the bridge. That was the last time they tried to shoot up Wichita's main street. Within two years, the worst violence had moved westward to Dodge City.

In the spring of 1876, Dodge City badly needed a strong lawman. Newspapers were calling it the wickedest cowtown in the West. The saloons were filled with cowboys, buffalo hunters, and railroad workers. Gamblers and thieves raked in the easy money. Gunfights were a nightly event.

Wyatt (left) hired Bat Masterson (right) as a lawman in Dodge City, Kansas. The pair remained friends for many years.

Mayor George Hoover hired Wyatt as the town marshal. Wyatt picked his brother Morgan as deputy. He also hired Bat Masterson and Bat's brother, Jim. Then he drew a line at the tracks that cut the town in half. Only lawmen were allowed to carry guns north of that line. Everyone else had to check his guns at racks set up in hotels, stores, and saloons. Wyatt and his deputies used their own guns only as a last resort. Bat patrolled the town's main street with a walking stick in his hand. Sometimes he used it to club drunken hoodlums.

The Dodge City police force made ten or more arrests a day. Some men went to jail with their heads bloodied by Wyatt's Buntline Special. At other times, Wyatt fought with his fists. In one fight, a cowboy tried to rake Wyatt with his spurs. The marshal sidestepped and punched the man in the stomach. A crowd pressed in to watch. Before the cowboy knew what was happening, Wyatt's second blow ended the fight. The marshal's shirt was still a spotless white.

When the cattle drives ended that fall, Wyatt took stock of his record. He had kept the peace in Dodge City for eight months. During that time, dozens of men spent time in the city jail. He and his deputies had collected thousands of dollars in fines. In keeping with custom, the lawmen split the fines among themselves.

When it came to shootings, only two men had been killed. That number compared to over seventy in the four years before Wyatt came to Dodge. Thanks to his cool leadership, the police had not killed anyone. Wyatt was given the credit for taming the rowdy cowtown.

When the cowboys returned to Texas, Dodge City quieted down. Restless as always, Wyatt decided to prospect for gold. With Morgan beside him, he headed north to the Dakotas.

Deadwood City was the center of the Black Hills gold strike. When he arrived, Wyatt learned that all the good claims had been taken. To make matters worse, the first snows were falling. Morgan hurried back to Dodge, but Wyatt stayed in Deadwood. Unlike many of the miners, he still had his horses with him. If he could not strike gold, Wyatt thought, he could at least "mine the miners."

Firewood was in short supply that winter. Seeing his chance, Wyatt rigged up a wagon box that could be pulled on runners or on wheels. Then he drove out to where he could buy wood for $2 a cord. Back in Deadwood, the miners lined up to pay $12 a cord. One man paid $100 for a night delivery. He needed the firewood to keep a poker game going. By the time spring came, Wyatt had $5,000 in his pocket.

When Wyatt left Deadwood, Wells Fargo hired him to guard the Cheyenne stagecoach. A guard was needed because the stage carried a fortune in gold. Wyatt, riding shotgun, took his place next to the driver. Along the way, two outlaw bands tried to stop the stage. When Wyatt calmly opened fire, the bandits gave up the chase.

Wyatt stayed on guard for the full 300-mile trip. Even though he had saved the gold, Wells Fargo paid him only $50. Stung by the low pay, Wyatt went looking for another job. In Cheyenne, a telegram was waiting. Would Wyatt hurry back to Dodge City? The cowboys were tearing up the town again.

CHAPTER FOUR

THE EARPS MOVE TO TOMBSTONE

Wyatt returned to Dodge City in 1877. Once again, he cracked down hard on the high-spirited Texas cowboys. Wyatt earned $2.50 for each arrest he made. In the first month, he collected nearly $1,000. Wyatt called it "taming the cowboys." Virgil and Morgan Earp hired on as his deputies.

Wyatt's strict rules angered the cowboys. So did his friendship with the hot-tempered Doc Holliday. Doc was a part-time dentist and full-time gambler.

Doc Holliday was a part-time dentist, a gambler, and a colorful character in Dodge City. He was also Wyatt's close friend.

Although he suffered from a lung disease, Doc was a crack shot. He was a good man to have on your side in a fight.

Word soon spread that Wyatt was in danger. The Texans, it was said, had offered a reward to anyone who killed the marshal. A gunslinger named Clay Allison gave it a try, but failed. Cool as always, Wyatt drove Allison out of town. Next, in July 1878, George Hoyt made his move. As he galloped along the main street, he took several wild shots at Wyatt. One bullet punched a hole in the marshal's hat. The two men then exchanged shots. When Hoyt tried to flee, Wyatt shot him off his horse. The lawman had killed his first man.

In September, Tobe Driskill and his cowboy friends rode into town at high speed. After shooting up Front Street, they stopped at a saloon for a drink. As he walked into the saloon, Driskill saw Wyatt standing at the bar. Before the marshal could reach his shotgun, Driskill and one of his pals drew on him.

It was a tight spot. If Wyatt made a move, they would surely shoot him. At that moment, Doc Holliday burst into the saloon with a six-gun in each hand. When the two gunmen turned to look at Doc, Wyatt drew his own Colt. Moving quickly, he knocked Driskill down. The second cowboy pointed his pistol at the marshal, but Doc's gun roared first. The Texan went down with a bullet in his shoulder. The rest of Driskill's friends raised their hands.

Wyatt handed in his badge in the fall of 1879. "I'm tired of being a target," he said. After leaving Dodge, he headed west. Virgil had told him about a silver strike in Tombstone, Arizona. The desert town was set on a rocky plateau named Goose Flats. Apache Indians roamed the nearby mountains. Like most frontier mining towns, Tombstone lived by the law of the six-gun. Outsiders often called it "the town too tough to die."

Skilled, hardworking law officers were in demand. Wyatt signed on as deputy sheriff and tax collector for Pima County. The pay was good, and he did not have

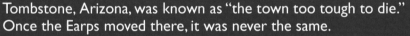

Tombstone, Arizona, was known as "the town too tough to die." Once the Earps moved there, it was never the same.

to patrol the streets. That meant he was less likely to be used for target practice. Virgil gave up looking for silver to work as a deputy town marshal. Morgan and Jim Earp soon joined their brothers. Morgan rode shotgun for Wells Fargo and Jim worked as a bartender.

Tombstone seemed to attract outlaws. The local gang leader was N. H. "Old Man" Clanton. Clanton lived on a ranch near Tombstone with his sons Ike, Phin, and Billy. He also kept some well-known gunmen on his payroll. They included Curly Bill Brocius, Frank Stilwell, Frank and Tom McLaury, and Johnny Ringo. When they were not holding up stagecoaches, the outlaws tended to their small ranches. They stocked the ranches with cattle stolen on their forays into Mexico. Old Man Clanton was killed on one of those raids.

The Clanton gang soon clashed with the Earps. In October 1880, Wyatt was helping Town Marshal Fred White arrest some drunks. When the lawmen looked up, they saw Curly Bill waving a loaded pistol. As White grabbed at the gun, it went off. The bullet slammed into his stomach. An instant later, Wyatt knocked Curly Bill flat with his pistol. Before he died, White said that the shooting was an accident. A judge fined Curly Bill and set him free.

The towns Wyatt "cleaned up" are highlighted on this 1872 map. Dakota territory would not be split into two states (North and South Dakota) until 1889.

A few months later, lawmakers divided Pima County. The split left Tombstone as part of the new Cochise County. A deputy U.S. marshal enforced federal laws there. A county sheriff policed the county land that lay outside the city limits. In Tombstone, a town marshal was charged with keeping the peace.

Virgil took over as town marshal. Wyatt wanted the job of county sheriff, but John Behan was named to the post. Wyatt, who was still a deputy marshal, did not trust Behan. The new sheriff was friendly with the outlaws who lived near Tombstone. He even hired some of them as deputies.

Doc Holliday arrived about this time. He was drawn by the gambling and his friendship with Wyatt. The Earps were glad to see him, because the Clantons were making trouble again. The feud heated up when Wyatt's best horse was stolen. He tracked the horse and found it—with Billy Clanton in the saddle. Wyatt took his mount back at gunpoint.

John Behan may have been the sheriff of Cochise County, but he was friendly with the outlaws in the area. He always sided with them against the Earps.

In January 1881, the Earps were tested by a lynch mob. The affair began when a gambler called Johnny-Behind-the-Deuce shot a miner. After Johnny was arrested, a mob formed to lynch him. Virgil and Morgan tried to hide their prisoner in a bowling alley. Wyatt, always ready to help his brothers, stood guard. When the mob surged forward he aimed his shotgun at one of the leaders. His target was Dick Gird, a mine owner who employed half of the men in the mob. Faced with that deadly shotgun, Gird turned and walked away. One by one, the other miners followed him.

In March, masked men fired on the Tucson stage, killing the driver. A quick-thinking guard picked up the reins and drove the stage to safety. When Wyatt heard the news, he set out with a posse to chase the killers. He soon caught up with Luther King, who named some Clanton men as his partners. After Wyatt took King to jail, Sheriff Behan let him escape. Behan then charged Doc Holliday with the robbery. He put Doc in jail, but had to let him go for lack of proof.

Six months later, a gang robbed the Bisbee stage. A witness heard one of the robbers say, "Have we got all the sugar?" Wyatt knew that Frank Stilwell, a Clanton man, often used that phrase. The boot tracks at the scene also pointed to Stilwell. He was arrested in Bisbee and returned to Tombstone.

Ike Clanton and Tom McLaury posted bail for their friend. Later, Tom met Morgan Earp on the street and offered to fight him. Morgan refused—for the moment. The stage was set for a final showdown.

CHAPTER FIVE

GUNFIGHT AT THE O.K. CORRAL

In the fall of 1881, the Clantons boasted that they would kill the Earps. Wyatt and his brothers heard the talk and stayed alert. Tombstone's leading citizens were worried. They feared that outlaws would take over the town if the Clantons won a shoot-out. They asked Marshal Virgil Earp to swear in Wyatt and Morgan as deputies.

Ike Clanton acted as though he owned the town. On October 25 he spent the night in the saloons, drinking and gambling. Doc Holliday saw him and tried to pick a fight. "Get out your gun and go to work," Doc snarled. The taunt failed. Because Ike was unarmed, Doc could not draw on him.

Ike stayed up all night playing poker. In the morning, half drunk, he armed himself with pistols and a rifle. As he walked the streets, he told everyone that the shooting was about to start. Virgil caught up with

Ike and put him under arrest. Ike tried to draw his six-gun, but Virgil used Wyatt's trick. He knocked Ike out with one swing of his pistol.

Wyatt caught up with Ike at the courtroom and told him to behave. Ike growled that he would take care of Wyatt later. Morgan locked up Ike's guns, and the outlaw paid his $25 fine. Billy Claibourne then took his boss to have his head bandaged.

Later, the Clantons and the McLaurys met near the O.K. Corral. Billy Clanton told Ike he should go back to the ranch. Ike said he would go, but not just yet. In the meantime, the Earps heard that the Clantons were spoiling for a fight. Wyatt told his brothers they could no longer avoid a showdown.

Ike Clanton was the ringleader in the feud with the Earp brothers. He and his gang boasted that they were going to kill the Earps.

Wyatt, Virgil, and Morgan set off on the long walk to the corral. The three tall lawmen were dressed in long black coats and black hats. Doc Holliday heard the news and rushed to join his friends. Wyatt told him that it was not his fight. That hurt Doc's feelings. Virgil stepped in, saying they would need Doc if the shooting started. He deputized Doc and gave him a shotgun to hide under his coat.

The four lawmen turned the corner onto Fremont Street. Now they could see the Clanton gang half a block away. The outlaws were standing near Fry's Photography Gallery. Sheriff Behan was with them, trying to talk them into giving up

Both Tom McLaury (above) and his brother Frank were killed in the gunfight at the O.K. Corral. They were members of the Clantons' gang.

their guns. Ike said he was unarmed and the others refused to listen to the sheriff.

As the Earps moved closer, Behan hurried toward them, begging them to stop. Virgil brushed the sheriff aside. At that point, Behan and Billy Claiborne hid inside Fry's Gallery. The Clantons and McLaurys waited with their backs against the house next door.

Soon the grim-faced men were only six feet apart. The Earps had the outlaws boxed in. Virgil ordered the four men to lay down their guns. Billy Clanton and Frank McLaury responded by cocking their pistols. In the next instant the shooting started.

Wyatt's first shot wounded Frank, who staggered into the street. Billy hurried his return shot and missed Wyatt. Morgan turned his gun on Billy, shooting him in the wrist and chest. Ike wrestled with Wyatt, but Wyatt pushed the unarmed man away. Ike scurried into Fry's Gallery. A moment later, he ran out the back door and fled. Tom McLaury was yelling that he was unarmed. He tried to grab a rifle from Frank's horse, but he was not fast enough. The horse reared, giving Doc time for one shot. A volley of shotgun pellets ripped through Tom's vest. He dragged himself away, only to collapse at the corner.

Billy and Frank were still firing from where they lay. One of Billy's bullets hit Virgil in the leg. Frank got off a shot that plugged Doc in the hip. A second later, Morgan put a slug just below Frank's ear. Billy turned his fire on Morgan and hit him in the shoulder. Then he tried to stand up, but Wyatt and Morgan cut him down. Even as Billy lay dying, he begged for more shells for his empty gun.

Although the battle lasted less than a minute, both McLaurys and Billy Clanton were dead. Virgil, Morgan, and Doc were bleeding from their wounds. As the smoke cleared, Sheriff Behan emerged from his

The shootout at the O.K. Corral has been portrayed many times. This scene is from the 1957 film *Gunfight at the O.K. Corral.* Actor Burt Lancaster (below) played Wyatt Earp.

hiding place. He charged the Earps and Doc Holliday with murder.

Public feeling in Tombstone was split. One side stood up for the Earps, the other backed Sheriff Behan. When the trial came it dragged on for a month. After hearing the testimony, Judge Wells Spicer ruled that the Earps had acted within the law. He said they had the right to defend themselves while doing their duty.

Virgil went back to his post as town marshal after his wound healed. One night, just after Christmas, he set out on patrol. Hidden by darkness, some gunmen opened fire on him with shotguns. Wyatt heard the gunfire and ran to the scene. He found Virgil bleeding from wounds in his thigh and left arm. A doctor had to remove four inches of bone from the arm. The injuries left Virgil with a crippled arm and a bad limp.

Wyatt was sure Ike Clanton and his friends had ambushed his brother. Ike laughed at the charges when he heard them. He had sixteen men lined up to swear he had not been near Tombstone that night. Sheriff Behan said he believed Ike's alibi. Virgil was too badly hurt to take a hand in the matter. He had to resign as marshal.

The town remained quiet for three months. In March 1882, Wyatt and Morgan spent an evening at the theater. Afterward, Morgan left to shoot some pool. Wyatt felt sleepy, but he had a hunch there might be trouble. He joined Morgan at the pool hall.

Three of Ike's men were in town that night. Pete Spence saw Wyatt and Morgan playing pool and told the others. Frank Stilwell, Spence, and Indian Charlie crept up to the back door. Suddenly the glass shattered as a six-gun blazed. The two bullets missed Wyatt, but Morgan was standing in the line of fire. One of the slugs hit him in the spine.

Some bystanders carried Morgan to a couch. "This is the last game of pool I'll ever play," he gasped.

A witness told Wyatt he had seen three men running away. As Wyatt watched his brother die, he swore an oath. The Clantons, he vowed, will pay with their blood for shooting Morgan.

After Morgan Earp (above) was killed by members of the Clanton gang, Wyatt vowed revenge.

CHAPTER SIX

TOMBSTONE AND BEYOND

On the Monday after Morgan's death, Wyatt put Virgil and his wife on a train. Virgil's wounds were still healing and Wyatt wanted him out of Tombstone. He then loaded Morgan's body onto the same train. Virgil said he would bury his brother in the Earp family plot in Colton, California.

Wyatt and Doc Holliday rode the train as far as Tucson. Word had reached them that Morgan's killers had been seen there. In their minds, the debt had to be paid in blood.

That night, Wyatt watched Virgil's train pull out of the Tucson station. As it gained speed, the train's headlamps revealed four men hiding in the shadows. Wyatt and Doc went after them. The men split up and ran. Wyatt, shotgun in hand, cornered one of them in the dark railway yard. The man was Frank Stilwell.

Stilwell did not draw his gun. Wyatt, blinded by his desire for revenge, did not seem to notice. He blasted Stilwell with the shotgun. "I let him have both barrels," he later told his lawyer. "I have no regrets. I know I got the man who killed Morg."

In Tombstone, Ike Clanton swore out a warrant against Wyatt and Doc. The legal paper charged them with Stilwell's murder. At the same time, Wyatt obtained a warrant of his own. It named Indian Charlie and Pete Spence as Morgan's killers.

Before long two posses were combing the desert around Tombstone. Sheriff Behan's posse was made up of Clanton men. Its job was to find and arrest Wyatt and Doc. Wyatt said he and the posse he led were there to rid the county of outlaws. If the two posses met there was certain to be gunplay.

Wyatt and his men tracked Indian Charlie to a water hole. Charlie tried to run for it, but Wyatt cut him down. That took care of two of Morgan's killers, he reckoned.

At this point, accounts differ. Some stories say that the two posses did shoot it out. If Wyatt's side was telling the truth, at least five slugs ripped through his hat. Unharmed by the hail of bullets, Wyatt then killed Curly Bill Brocius with his shotgun. The anti-Earp accounts disagree. They say that Curly Bill was nowhere near Tombstone at the time. More to the point, this version claims that the two posses never met.

For Wyatt and Doc the game was over. They had to leave Tombstone. Friends told them that Sheriff Behan planned to arrest them. Once you're in jail, they warned, you

When Wyatt and Doc Holliday fled Arizona in 1882, they headed to Colorado. Their old friend Bat Masterson (above) owned a gambling hall there.

will never get out alive. Wyatt and Doc did not argue the point. They packed up and headed north to Colorado.

Wyatt's friend Bat Masterson owned a gambling hall in Gunnison, Colorado. Bat talked to Governor Pitkin about Wyatt and Doc. Pitkin agreed that sending the pair back to Tombstone would mean certain death. When the request came to extradite Doc, Pitkin turned it down.

Far away from Tombstone, Wyatt started a new life. He and Doc split up, although they remained good friends. Doc died in bed of his lung ailment five years later in 1887. Wyatt also left Mattie Blaylock behind. He had lived with Mattie in Tombstone, but had not married her. Now he went back to the card tables. As skilled with cards as with a gun, he rode out of Gunnison with $10,000 in his pocket.

Wyatt was still as footloose as always. He searched for gold, but without success. Drifting on to California, he turned to real estate. San Diego was booming, and for two years Wyatt made money buying and selling land there. Moving north, he began to buy racehorses. Using his farm near San Jose as a base, he ran his horses at racetracks on both coasts.

Wyatt's name made headlines again in 1894. The Southern Pacific Railroad was having labor troubles. Fearful that its pay train would be held up, the railroad hired Wyatt as a guard. The train's route ran from Oakland, California, to El Paso, Texas. With Wyatt riding shotgun in the cab of the locomotive, no one tried to rob the train. The payroll money went through safely.

Wyatt was offered the post of U.S. marshal for Arizona that same year. The offer surprised him.

Wyatt made a good living in Alsaka as a saloon keeper. He had also owned a saloon in Tombstone called the Oriental (above, with Wyatt standing at right).

Wasn't he wanted for murder there? Now he learned that the old charges had been dropped. Even so, Wyatt turned down the job. He knew that young gunmen would try to win fame by shooting him. A marshal should keep the peace, not cause more deaths, he said.

Wyatt was still hoping for a big strike. When gold was found in the Klondike in 1897, he headed for Alaska. He did not strike it rich, but he knew other ways to make money. Nome was a city of tents when Wyatt built the first wooden building there. The Dexter Saloon was soon turning a nice profit.

For much of this time, Wyatt lived with Josephine "Josie" Marcus. Wyatt had first met the actress in Tombstone. She had been Sheriff Behan's girl, but it was Wyatt who won her heart. Josie was half Wyatt's age, but his match in courage. When Wyatt went into the California desert to look for gold, Josie went with him. Some experts say the couple never wed. Josie said they married when they returned from Alaska.

The Earps finally struck it rich in the Colorado River valley. Their claim there turned into the Happy Day gold and copper mines. With the mines earning good money, luck smiled on Wyatt once more. A drilling rig hit oil on his land in central California.

Wyatt settled down to a quiet life, managing his mines and oil wells. His doctor reported that the old gunslinger's body did not show a single bullet scar. One by one, his parents and his brothers died. Only one sister outlived him.

Death came when Wyatt Earp was eighty years old. He died in Josie's arms on January 13, 1929, in Los Angeles. Josie buried his ashes in her family plot in Colma, California. Today, the old lawman's name lives on as an enduring hero of the Wild West.

The legendary Wyatt Earp lived to be eighty years old. This picture was taken in 1926, three years before his death.

CHAPTER SEVEN

THE LEGEND OF WYATT EARP

Wyatt Earp's fame has continued to grow since his death. Most of the books and all of the TV shows and movies about him were produced after 1929. His friends said Wyatt wanted his story to be told. That was why the old marshal worked with Stuart Lake on a book about his life. Lake later published the book under the title, *Wyatt Earp: Frontier Marshal.* Although the book was more fiction than fact, readers loved it.

How much of Wyatt's fame is based on fact? As is often the case, there are two sides to the story. His critics point out that he was a lawman for only ten years. Also, would an honest lawman own saloons and gambling halls? They further charge him with a number of killings. Wyatt did, in fact, leave Tombstone with a murder charge hanging over him.

Through the years, Wyatt Earp's legend has grown. In the 1990s, the film *Wyatt Earp* was a huge hit. Actor Kevin Costner (above) portrayed him in that 1994 movie.

A close look at the record clears Wyatt of most charges. In the cowtowns of the Old West, a ten-year career as a lawman was a lifetime. More to the point, Wyatt brought law and order with him when he came to town. Crime rates tumbled during the months he patrolled the streets of Wichita and Dodge City. As for his investments, many early lawmen owned saloons and gambling halls. Wyatt saw no reason to turn his back when there was a profit to be made.

The charge that Wyatt enjoyed killing is the most unjust of all. At a time when gunplay was the rule, he was seldom quick on the trigger. Instead of shooting rowdy cowboys he often knocked them over the head with his Buntline Special. Wyatt did not believe in peace at any price, however. After Morgan was gunned down, he took a bloody revenge on the men who fired the fatal shots.

The Old West had its fair share of able, hardworking lawmen. Wyatt Earp was more colorful and more skillful than most. Despite his failings, Wyatt earned his fame fairly. If you were in danger, he was a good man to have on your side.

GLOSSARY

ambush—A surprise attack.

bail—Money paid to a court to guarantee the return of a suspect for trial.

Civil War—The war fought between the North (the Union) and the South (the Confederacy), 1861–1865.

claims—Tracts of land that western settlers and miners staked out as their own.

cord of wood—A stack of firewood that measures 4x4x8 feet.

corral—A fenced area where ranchers keep horses or cattle.

deputy—A lawman who assists a sheriff or marshal.

dime novels—Low-cost magazines that printed popular fiction during the late 1800s.

extradite—To return a suspected criminal to another state to stand trial.

frontier—A region that is being opened to settlement. Life on the western frontier was often hard and dangerous.

gunslingers—Outlaws and lawmen of the Old West who settled arguments with their pistols.

legend—A story that many people believe, but which is often untrue in whole or in part.

lynch mob—An out-of-control crowd that is intent on hanging someone.

Mexican War—The war between the United States and Mexico, 1846–1848.

plateau—A large, flat land area that rises sharply above the surrounding terrain.

posse—A group of citizens who join with lawmen to aid in the capture of outlaws.

prospect—To explore a region in search of natural resources, such as gold.

town council—A group of citizens elected to run a local government.

typhus—A disease carried by fleas. In the 1800s, people who fell ill of typhus often died.

Union—The name given to the Northern states that fought against the South during the Civil War.

warrant—A legal paper that gives a lawman the right to arrest someone for a crime.

FURTHER READING

Books

Briggs, Robert. *Hurled Into Eternity: The Story of the Earps in Tombstone, 1880–1882.* Madison, Ga.: Southern Lion Books, 2007.

Goodman, Michael E. *Wyatt Earp.* Mankato, Minn.: Creative Education, 2005.

Landau, Elaine. *Wyatt Earp: Wild West Lawman.* Berkeley Heights, N.J.: Enslow, 2004.

Urban, William L. *Wyatt Earp: The OK Corral and the Law of the American West.* New York: Rosen Publishing Group, 2003.

Internet Addresses

Spartacus Educational: Wyatt Earp
http://www.spartacus.schoolnet.co.uk/WWearpW.htm

Wyatt Earp History Page
http://www.wyattearp.net

INDEX